50 &

Over the Hill

T'was the eve of my Fiftieth...

T'was the eve of my 50th
when lo and behold
I glanced in the mirror and said
OH NO, I'M OLD!!!

It seems only yesterday
I had all my teeth,

**now Milk of Magnesia
is my daily relief!**

I think I remember when I was a child
all I wanted to do was grow up and be wild.

Now that I'm here I don't see the big deal
my cane and bifocals have little appeal.

My reflexes are failing
causing added dismay.

I can't seem to use enough Oil of Olay.

My bones make loud noise, and what's more I've been thinking,

my waist is expanding,
my height is now shrinking!

My vision is failing and my hearing is shot.

And I really do visit the john quite a lot!

I get cranky and
yell at the drop of a hat,

and sometimes when driving
I forget where I'm at!

I don't like to dance or
loud music to boot.
I just like the quiet and
don't give a hoot!

I walk with a shuffle as
I go down the hall,

My afternoon naps
have become an obsession.

Is there any relief for my state of depression?

My arches have fallen, my hair is a mess,

I'd rather sit home on my duff I confess!

I slouch in my chair,
my socks rolled to my ankles
searching for something
to help me feel thankful.

I guess there is really
no sense in denying,
I'm going down hill and
my brain cells are dying!

Before I dose off
I would like to explain
that being an old fart
is not really a pain...

There's surely one good thing
that getting old does...
Just wish I could remember
WHAT THE HECK it was!!!

THE END